# I CAN BE AN ARTIST

By Alex Appleby

Gareth Stevens
PUBLISHING

Please visit our website, www.garethstevens.com. For a free color catalog of all our high-quality books, call toll free 1-800-542-2595 or fax 1-877-542-2596.

Library of Congress Cataloging-in-Publication Data

Appleby, Alex.
I can be an artist / by Alex Appleby.
p. cm. — (When I grow up)
Includes index.
ISBN 978-1-4824-0752-5 (pbk.)
ISBN 978-1-4824-0827-0 (6-pack)
ISBN 978-1-4824-0751-8 (library binding)
1. Artists — Vocational guidance — Juvenile literature. 2. Artists — Juvenile literature. I. Appleby, Alex. II. Title.
N8350.A66 2014
709—d23

First Edition

Published in 2015 by
**Gareth Stevens Publishing**
111 East 14th Street, Suite 349
New York, NY 10003

Copyright © 2015 Gareth Stevens Publishing

Editor: Ryan Nagelhout
Designer: Sarah Liddell

Photo credits: Cover, p. 1 Sergey Nivens/Shutterstock.com; p. 5 © iStockphoto.com/anatols; p. 7 Helder Almeida/Shutterstock.com; pp. 9, 11, 17 Africa Studio/Shutterstock.com; p. 13 Sushaaa/Shutterstock.com; p. 15 Ingrid Balabanova/Shutterstock.com; p. 19 racorn/Shutterstock.com; p. 21 Monkey Business Images/Shutterstock.com; p. 23 © iStockphoto.com/Wavebreak; p. 24 (colored pencils) Gayvoronskaya_Yana/Shutterstock.com.

Printed in the United States of America

CPSIA compliance information: Batch #CS15GS: For further information contact Gareth Stevens, New York, New York at 1-800-542-2595.

# Contents

I want to be an artist!

I love to make things.

I make things with clay.

I also love to paint.

I mix my paints
with water.

I use many
different colors.

I can draw, too.

I like to use
colored pencils.

I like to take art classes.

I want to go to art school when I grow up.

# Words to Know

clay

colored pencils

# Index